ESSENTIAL ENERGY

NUCLEAR ENERGY

Robert Snedden

Heinemann
LIBRARY

www.heinemann.co.uk/library

To order:
☎ Phone 44 (0) 1865 888112
🖹 Send a fax to 44 (0) 1865 314091
🖥 Visit the Heinemann bookshop at www.heinemann.co.uk/library to browse our catalogue and order online.

First published in Great Britain by Heinemann Library,
Halley Court, Jordan Hill, Oxford OX2 8EJ, part of Harcourt Education.
Heinemann is a registered trademark of Harcourt Education Ltd.

Editorial: Clare Lewis
Design: David Poole and Damco Solutions Ltd
Illustrations: Jeff Edwards
Picture Research: Maria Joannou
Production: Helen McCreath

Originated by Chroma Graphics
Printed and bound in WKT Company Ltd in China

10 digit ISBN 0 431 11772 1
10 09 08 07 06

13 digit ISBN 978 0 431 11772 0
10 9 8 7 6 5 4 3 2 1

British Library Cataloguing in Publication Data
Snedden, Robert
Nuclear Energy – 2nd Ed – (Essential Energy)
333.7'924
A full catalogue record for this book is available from the British Library.

Acknowledgements
The publishers would like to thank the following for permission to reproduce photographs:
Camera Press: Pg.13; Corbis: Pg.5, Pg.11, Pg.14, Pg.28; Environmental Images: Pg.4, Pg.22, Pg.24, Pg.30, Pg.31, Pg.36; Landauer: Pg.34; Popperfoto: Pg.39, Pg.42, Pg.43; Robert Harding Picture Library: Pg.18; Science Photo Library: Pg.8, Pg.12, Pg.15, Pg.17, Pg.20, Pg.23, Pg.25, Pg.26, Pg.27, Pg.29, Pg.32, Pg.33, Pg.37, Pg.41.

Cover photograph of a nuclear explosion, reproduced with permission of Corbis.

The publishers would like to thank Helen Lloyd for her assistance in the preparation of this book.

CONTENTS

Nuclear power? No thanks?..4

Inside the atom..6

Energy from the atom 8

Neutrons and chain reactions 10

Unlocking the atom 12

Uranium mining..14

Producing nuclear fuels 16

Inside a nuclear power station...18

Control and containment..20

Reactor systems 22

Fast breeders, fast movers 24

Spent fuel and reprocessing 26

Dealing with nuclear waste..28

Disposal dilemma...30

Radiation and life 32

Dosage and damage 34

Reactor accidents...36

Chernobyl and beyond 38

Nuclear future..40

Nuclear weapons..42

Timeline 44

International Nuclear Event Scale...45

Find out more...45

Glossary 46

Index 48

Any words appearing in the text in bold, **like this** are explained in the glossary.

NUCLEAR POWER?
NO THANKS?

At the beginning of the 20th century no one dreamed that there could be such a thing as nuclear power. Scientists were just beginning to discover **radioactivity** and taking its first steps towards discovering how **atoms**, the particles from which all matter is made, are put together. In 1905 Albert Einstein, in his "theory of relativity", showed that **mass** could be changed into energy, and vice versa. By 1918 Sir Ernest Rutherford had shown that atoms could be split, and by 1942 the world had its first nuclear **reactor**.

In the late 20th century nuclear power was the second biggest source of energy for the industrialized world. The number one source of energy is still **fossil fuels**. For many people, **nuclear energy** was the answer to the problem of diminishing fossil fuel resources and the pollution caused by burning fossil fuels. There was talk of the possibility of nuclear power providing electricity "too cheap to meter". But today the nuclear industry has stopped growing. Germany, for example, announced in June 2000 that it would phase out all its nuclear power plants and many other countries including Austria, Italy, and the Philippines have done the same. Britain has said that it will shut down all its old Magnox power stations. So what's wrong with nuclear power?

■ Anti-nuclear protestors demonstrated for a month against the Superphénix reactor in France.

Reactor reactions

Many people are concerned about the environmental and health aspects of nuclear power. Nuclear reactors produce **radiation**, which is harmful to living things. However, with or without nuclear power, radiation is a fact of life. It comes from the Sun, from rocks, from medical X-rays, and even from television sets. High doses of radiation can kill very quickly, and small doses (such as might leak from a normally operating nuclear plant) could build up over many years and also cause damage. Some scientists estimate that the average person gets five times as much radiation in a lifetime from sitting in front of the television or a computer monitor as they would from living near a nuclear power station.

Nuclear power is also objected to by many because of the connection with nuclear weapons. The risk of accidents, such as fires or explosions, could result in **radioactive** materials being released inside the power station and possibly outside as well. Government regulators in the United States have estimated that there is about a 50 per cent chance of a core **meltdown** in a US reactor within a 20-year period. Disposing of the hazardous waste that is the by-product of nuclear power is also a problem.

■ Reactor number one at Calder Hall, Cumbria – Britain's
first nuclear power station – opened in October 1956.

INSIDE THE ATOM

To understand how nuclear power works, we first have to take a look at the way **atoms** are put together. Atoms are the tiny particles from which all the materials around you are made. An atom can be divided into two parts. First there is an outer cloud of tiny particles called **electrons**. The number of electrons in the outermost part of this cloud determines how the atom will react with other atoms in chemical reactions.

The inner part of the atom is called the **nucleus**. This consists of a tightly packed cluster of particles called **protons** and **neutrons**. Each **element** has a different number of protons and neutrons, ranging from hydrogen, the simplest element, which has a single proton, to uranium, used as a nuclear fuel, which can have 235 or more protons and neutrons. Some elements can have even more particles in their nuclei. The atoms of a particular element all have the same number of protons in their nuclei – this is called the **atomic number**. The protons and neutrons take no part in chemical reactions.

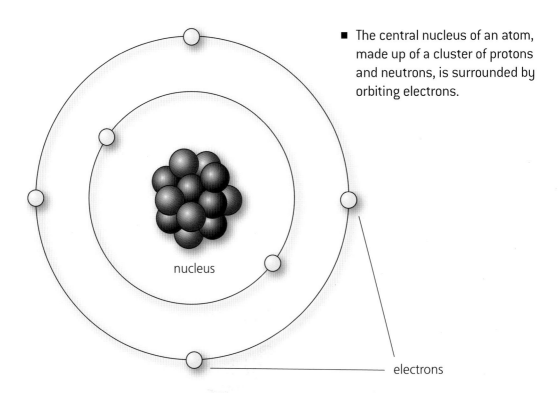

■ The central nucleus of an atom, made up of a cluster of protons and neutrons, is surrounded by orbiting electrons.

nucleus

electrons

Isotopes

It is possible for two or more atoms to have the same atomic number (the same number of protons), which means they are the same element, but have different numbers of neutrons. Such atoms are called **isotopes** of that element. Isotopes may be stable or **radioactive**, and may be naturally occurring or made in a laboratory. For example, carbon has the isotopes C12 (which is stable) and C14 (which is radioactive). The term was coined by English chemist Frederick Soddy, who was a pioneer researcher in atomic disintegration.

Radioactive elements

Of the known elements, 92 occur in nature. These elements have atomic numbers ranging from 1 (hydrogen) to 92 (uranium). Of these elements, 81 are stable; all the others, which include atomic numbers 43 (technetium), 61 (promethium), and from 84 (polonium) up to 92 (uranium), are radioactive.

A radioactive substance is one in which the nuclei of its atoms are unstable. They break apart, giving out energy as they do so. When the nucleus breaks up, or **decays**, it forms a nucleus that is more stable than it was before. The new nucleus may have fewer protons than the original, which means that it has become a different element. A radioactive element may go through several stages of decay before finally becoming a stable element.

HALF-LIFE

There is no way to predict when any one radioactive nucleus will decay. However, it is possible to say that half of the atoms in a particular sample of a radioactive material will have decayed by a certain time. This is called the radioactive element's **half-life**. Each radioactive isotope has a different half-life. These can range from a tiny fraction of a second to billions of years. The half-life of uranium 238 is about the same as the age the Earth is now, 4.5 billion years, whereas that of polonium 213 is just over four millionths of a second.

ENERGY FROM THE ATOM

An **element** is a substance that cannot be split chemically into simpler substances. Elements can react together in chemical reactions. All chemical reactions involve the release or the taking up of **chemical energy.** For instance, when coal is burnt, the carbon in the coal combines with oxygen to become carbon dioxide, and energy is released as heat. The **atoms** involved in a chemical reaction remain unchanged.

In contrast, the elements involved in a nuclear reaction can change as a result of it. In a nuclear reaction, an unstable atomic **nucleus** breaks up or **decays**. As it does so it releases radioactivity in the form of alpha, beta, and **gamma radiation**. A large unstable nucleus can also release **neutrons** as it decays.

Missing mass

No **mass** is ever lost when a chemical reaction takes place. The mass of the atoms present before the reaction will always equal the mass after the reaction. However, if you add up the mass of all the particles formed by the decay of an unstable nucleus, you will find that it is less than the mass of the original nucleus. So where is the missing mass?

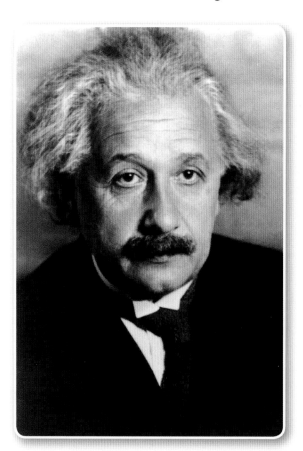

$E = mc^2$

As part of his theory of relativity, Albert Einstein showed that mass (m) and energy (E) were related by the equation $E = mc^2$, where c = the speed of light. In a nuclear reaction mass is converted into energy. The Sun, for example, produces an enormous amount of energy from nuclear reactions in its core that convert hydrogen into helium. In the process, the Sun loses four million tonnes of mass every second!

■ Albert Einstein (1879–1955), whose theory of relativity revealed the connection between matter and energy

Every time a nucleus breaks apart energy is released. In fact, the amount of energy released is massive. A given mass of uranium can provide 2.5 million times more energy than would be obtained by burning the same mass of carbon.

Most of the energy is in the form of kinetic (movement) energy as the nucleus flies apart. This kinetic energy is rapidly converted into **heat energy** as the fragments of the nucleus collide with other atoms. It is this heat that is used to generate electricity in a nuclear power station. Some of the remaining energy is carried off in the form of radioactive decay.

RADIOACTIVE DECAY

When the nucleus of a **radioactive** element breaks down it can emit different types of radioactivity.

- **Alpha particles** (α) are made up of two **protons** and two neutrons. This is the same as the nucleus of a helium atom. They are fast moving but can be stopped by a sheet of paper and will not travel far through the air.
- **Beta particles** (β) are fast moving **electrons**. They are more difficult to stop than alpha particles but can be halted by a thin sheet of metal.
- **Gamma rays** (γ) are not particles; they are a form of electromagnetic **radiation** with a very short wavelength and therefore a lot of energy. **Gamma radiation** is not easy to stop – a thick sheet of lead is needed to block gamma rays.

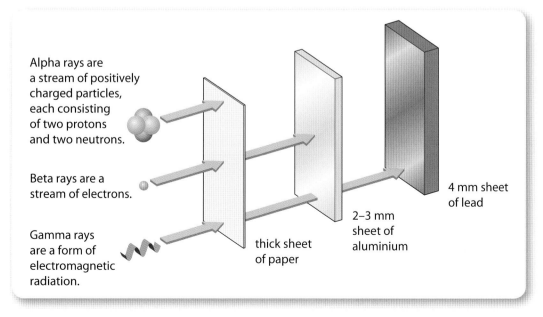

Alpha rays are a stream of positively charged particles, each consisting of two protons and two neutrons.

Beta rays are a stream of electrons.

Gamma rays are a form of electromagnetic radiation.

thick sheet of paper

2–3 mm sheet of aluminium

4 mm sheet of lead

■ The penetrating power of radioactivity

NEUTRONS AND CHAIN REACTIONS

Naturally occurring uranium contains two **isotopes**, U238, which makes up 99.28 per cent, and U235, which makes up the other 0.72 per cent. Uranium 235 is a fissile material. This means that if a U235 **nucleus** is struck by a **neutron** it will **fission**, or break apart. Neutrons striking U238 nuclei will simply be scattered. As the U235 nucleus breaks apart it releases energy and two or three more neutrons, which can then break up more U235 nuclei. These neutrons travel at around 20,000 kilometres (12,400 miles) per second – about 25,000 times faster than a space shuttle orbiting Earth! Because these neutrons can set off a **chain reaction**, they make it possible to obtain a continuous supply of energy from uranium.

■ The fission of a uranium atom.

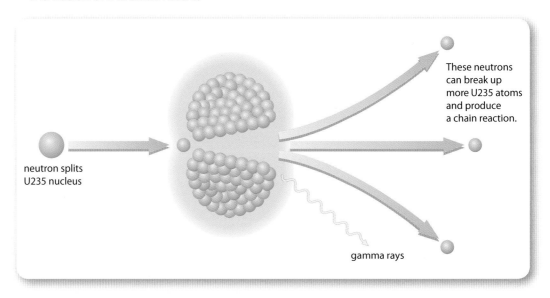

These neutrons can break up more U235 atoms and produce a chain reaction.

neutron splits U235 nucleus

gamma rays

Chain reactions

In a chain reaction the neutrons released by the fissioning uranium will strike other nuclei. When they strike U235 nuclei these will fission, too, releasing still more neutrons. These neutrons can go on to strike yet more nuclei, which will release yet more neutrons, and so the reaction continues. To increase the chances of neutrons striking U235, the uranium used in nuclear power stations is enriched, making the U235 content greater than it is normally.

There is no single chain reaction taking place. Within a typical nuclear power station there may be about a hundred million million million fission chain reactions taking place at any time.

The new nuclei formed when an unstable nucleus **decays** are called fission products. A uranium 235 atom becomes an atom of xenon and an atom of strontium. These new atoms are themselves unstable and will decay further.

The rate at which chain reactions take place can be controlled by introducing neutron-absorbing materials, such as **boron**, into the **reactor**. The fewer neutrons there are flying around, the fewer fissions there will be. Nuclear reactors use control rods to raise and lower the power output of the reactor.

■ The power of the atom is unleashed in the first detonation of an atomic bomb.

CRITICAL MASS

Neutrons reaching the surface of a reactor core can leak out, rather than trigger further fissions. The smaller the core, the greater the proportion of neutrons that leak out. The minimum amount of a fissile material that can maintain a continuous chain reaction is known as the critical **mass**. A reactor in which continuous chain reactions are taking place is said to be critical. If the amount of fissile material is much above the critical mass the reaction may accelerate uncontrollably. This is called a supercritical system – it is what happens in a nuclear explosion.

UNLOCKING THE ATOM

In the early part of the 20th century a number of researchers around the world were investigating what happens when **neutrons** strike uranium **atoms**. In 1938 German scientists Otto Hahn and Fritz Strassmann showed that when uranium is bombarded with neutrons, new, lighter **elements** are formed. A year later, Lise Meitner and Otto Frisch coined the term **fission** to describe this process, saying that what happened when the uranium was struck by neutrons was that it split, or fissioned, into lighter elements.

Developing weapons

The outbreak of World War II provided the spur to explore the uses of fission as a source of energy, particularly in the creation of weapons. The development of a weapon required not only that a self-sustaining fission reaction could be created, but also that a sufficient quantity of fissionable material could be produced for use in a weapon.

The United States government poured a colossal amount of money and resources into what was named the Manhattan Project. A team lead by Enrico Fermi succeeded in making the first nuclear **reactor** self-sustaining, or critical, at the University of Chicago on 2 December 1942. The reactor used natural uranium embedded in graphite blocks as its fuel.

■ The world's second nuclear reactor built at the Argonne Forest laboratory, Chicago, in 1943.

As we have seen, only the U235 **isotope** fissions, and natural uranium only contains 0.7 per cent of U235. To make a bomb, much higher concentrations of U235 are necessary. Part of the Manhattan Project's aim was to develop a way of separating U235 from U238. The solution was gaseous diffusion. You can read more about this technique on page 16.

Another way to develop weapons is to use a different fissile **nucleus**. An isotope of plutonium, Pu239, is formed when U238 reacts with neutrons to produce U239, which **decays** in two steps to produce Pu239. This Pu239 can be used in the manufacture of weapons. Once Fermi had demonstrated that a reactor could be built, the focus turned to building reactors to produce plutonium. The first such reactor was constructed in Oak Ridge, Tennessee. It took less than three years to develop this entirely new technology and it prepared the way for the development of **nuclear energy** for commercial use.

"Atoms for Peace"

The **Atomic Energy** Commission (AEC) was set up in 1946 to oversee civilian uses of nuclear power in the United States. In December 1953, in a speech at the United Nations, US President Eisenhower announced his decision to make nuclear-related information available to other countries in order to develop peaceful applications for nuclear energy. He called this 'atoms for peace'. The first international conference on nuclear energy was held in Geneva in 1955. Britain began production of nuclear-fuelled electricity in 1956. The first Soviet nuclear power plant came on line in 1954, and the French began construction of their first commercial plants in 1957. By the early 1960s nuclear power was firmly established as a commercial energy source.

■ US President Eisenhower supported the use of nuclear power for peaceful, domestic uses such as the production of electricity.

URANIUM MINING

The first stage in the nuclear fuel process is the mining of uranium ore (rock in which uranium is found). Uranium is one of the less common **elements**, although it is about 20 times more common than a precious metal, such as silver. Mining takes place at sites where the concentration of uranium is greater than about 0.04 per cent. Below this, extraction would cost too much.

Uranium is usually found as uraninite, an **oxide** of uranium, also known as pitchblende. The uranium is separated by first crushing the rock and then treating it with chemicals. The uranium leaves the mine as yellowcake, or uranium concentrate, another oxide of uranium. As the uranium concentrations are generally very low, a great deal of waste is produced when uranium is extracted from its ore. Even a high-concentration ore will still contain only about one per cent uranium. For every tonne (ton) of ore processed, 990 kilograms (2200 pounds) is waste.

HOW MUCH URANIUM?

Like **fossil fuels**, uranium is a non-renewable resource. There is only a limited amount available but how long it will last is influenced by a number of factors. For example, the use of uranium will decline if nuclear power is gradually phased out, in which case the reserves will last for considerably longer. Another possibility is that uranium currently stored in nuclear weapons could become available for power generation if these weapons were decommissioned.

■ A uranium mine in Australia.

The risks of mining

Uranium is **radioactive** – and **radioactivity** poses health hazards for people exposed to high levels of it. All of the various **isotopes** that uranium forms as it **decays** will be present in the ore. Because these are different **elements** they will be chemically different from uranium and so will form part of the waste material. The waste products left behind after the uranium has been extracted, called tailings, can be covered with earth or returned underground to reduce the risk of **radiation** exposure.

One of these wastes is a radioactive isotope of the gas, radon. This is released from the waste material. If it is inhaled it can cause damage to the inside of the lungs as it decays. In underground uranium mines the radon tends to accumulate. Miners used to call the lung diseases they developed from breathing radioactive dust "mountain sickness".

Cutting the risks, raising the costs

The average dose of radiation received by miners increases their risk of developing lung cancer by six times. The Union of Concerned Scientists in the United States says that radon levels can be reduced simply by ventilating the mines. They estimated that the cost of bringing exposure down to reasonably safe levels would be between 10 and 20 per cent of the value of the uranium mined.

■ A sample "button" of uranium 235, the fuel for nuclear reactors.

Unfortunately, mines that did this could become less profitable. This is just one of the ethical issues raised by the nuclear power industry. If the power stations buy their uranium from the cheapest source they are, in effect, discouraging mines from increasing safety for the miners, because increasing safety raises the cost of the uranium they produce. Often, the choice for workers in uranium mines is between risky work and no work at all.

PRODUCING NUCLEAR FUELS

Yellowcake is the raw material for nuclear fuel production. Basically, it is impure uranium trioxide and when purified it is a free-flowing orange-yellow powder. The next stage involves heating the uranium trioxide in a stream of hydrogen gas at a temperature of 650°C (1202°F). This gives chocolate brown uranium dioxide. A couple of **reactor** types can use uranium in this form as a fuel, but most use uranium dioxide that has been enriched to contain a higher proportion of U235.

Enriching uranium

There are two methods of enriching uranium. They both involve first heating the uranium dioxide with hydrogen fluoride gas to give lime-green uranium tetrafluoride. This is heated in fluorine gas to give uranium hexafluoride gas.

Gas diffusion

The first method relies on the fact that lighter **molecules** of a gas will **diffuse** through a porous material faster than heavier molecules. This means that molecules of uranium hexafluoride that contain U235 **atoms** will diffuse faster than molecules containing the heavier U238 atoms. This process has to be repeated many times before the uranium becomes significantly enriched. After being passed once through the porous material it may only be 1.004 times richer in U235 than before. This method requires a great deal of energy and the preferred way of enriching uranium is the second method.

FUEL PRODUCTION HAZARDS

The biggest hazards of nuclear fuel production come not from possible exposure to **radiation**, but from the chemicals used in the fuel processing. Fluorine and hydrogen fluoride are extremely hazardous chemicals. Fluorine, in fact, is the most reactive of all chemicals and both it and hydrogen fluoride can cause severe burns if they come into contact with unprotected skin. Hydrofluoric acid, a solution of hydrogen fluoride in water, penetrates deep into the skin tissues, but it may be several hours before pain develops and the destruction of the tissues begins.

■ A gas diffusion nuclear fuel
enrichment plant in Kentucky, USA

Gas centrifuge enrichment

In the second method the uranium hexafluoride is spun in a cylinder at around 1000 revolutions per second. The U238-containing molecules tend to move towards the wall of the container more readily, leaving the lighter U235 molecules in the centre. This separation is far from perfect, however, as gas molecules are always on the move and tend to mix again. However, gas removed from the centre will be richer in U235 by between 1.05 and 1.3 times, which is an improvement on 1.004! An enrichment plant will have a sequence of stages, called an enrichment cascade, and will have several hundred cascades running at the same time. Once the uranium hexafluoride has been enriched it is converted back into uranium dioxide by heating it with hydrogen and steam.

Gas centrifuge enrichment plants are smaller and less expensive to operate than gas diffusion plants. Enriched uranium dioxide provides the fuel for most of the world's nuclear reactors.

INSIDE A NUCLEAR POWER STATION

Many of the features of a nuclear power station are similar to those of other power stations. A source of fuel (coal, gas, or oil in a **fossil fuel** station) is used to provide energy to heat water and so produce high-energy steam to spin a **turbine**. The mechanical energy of the turbine is used to generate electricity. The steam is turned back into liquid water and recycled to the steam generator.

The reactor core

The heart of a nuclear power station is the **reactor** core. This is where the nuclear fuel is held and where it undergoes **fission** to produce energy. The fuel is in the form of a stack of pellets or a cylindrical rod held in a thin-walled metal container, called **cladding**. The rods and cladding together are called **fuel rods**. In most reactors a fuel element consists of several fuel rods bundled together with spaces between them through which coolants can flow. There will be 200 or more fuel elements in a typical reactor. A fuel element will produce energy for three to six years before it has to be replaced.

■ A worker changes fuel rods in a nuclear power station in Switzerland.

Coolants

The gas or liquid coolant passes through the reactor core and carries the heat away to the steam generators. The coolant comes into contact with the cladding, not directly with the nuclear fuel. A coolant has to be selected carefully: it must not react chemically with the cladding, it must not absorb too many **neutrons** because this would slow down the **chain reactions**, and it should be inexpensive. The majority of reactors use carbon dioxide and helium gases, and light and heavy water. (Light water is ordinary everyday water; heavy water has an **isotope** of hydrogen in which the hydrogen **atom** has a neutron in its **nucleus** as well as a **proton**.)

The heated gas is pumped to generators where steam is produced. If light water is used it may be allowed to boil, so producing steam directly. This is called a direct steam cycle. If heavy water is used, it may heat a separate water supply – an indirect steam cycle. The coolant is pumped back to the reactor after it has been used to heat the steam.

Moderators

A **moderator** is a substance that slows down neutrons so they have a greater chance of striking fissile U235 nuclei. The moderator surrounds the fuel rods. It is generally a material such as graphite or heavy water.

Pressure vessels and shielding

The coolant in a nuclear reactor is kept under pressure, and for this reason the reactor core is surrounded by a pressure vessel.

It is of great importance that the people working in a nuclear power plant are shielded from harmful **radiation**. The pressure vessel gives some protection, but an additional shield is also required for most reactors. This is called the biological shield, or just simply "the shield". The shield has to be thick enough to protect the workers from neutrons and **gamma radiation** at all times. Concrete is a very good shielding material and typically a thickness of about two to three metres surrounds the reactor.

CONTROL AND CONTAINMENT

Several steps are taken to ensure that **radioactive** materials stay within the **reactor**. The **cladding** keeps the **fission** products in the **fuel rods**, but if they do escape they will enter the coolant. The coolant flows in a closed loop around the reactor and so fission products should not escape into the environment.

However, if there is a leak in the coolant circuit then **radioactivity** will escape. The radioactivity will then reach another barrier to prevent it from spreading into the outside world, and that is the reactor building itself, called the reactor containment building.

Reactor control

The **chain reactions** in a nuclear reactor can be controlled by introducing into the reactor materials that absorb **neutrons**. This is done by using control rods made of a neutron-absorber, such as **boron** or cadmium. These rods can be moved in and out of the reactor as necessary. If the reactor is critical, meaning there is a continuous self-sustaining series of chain reactions in progress, it can be shut down, or made subcritical, by introducing control rods. The reactor can be started up again by simply removing the rods. The control rods need not be actual rods of material. Some reactors use a neutron-absorbing liquid or gas as part of their shutdown system.

■ Nuclear reactor control rods. These are inserted into the reactor core to absorb neutrons and slow down the chain reactions.

A reactor will typically have 50 or more control rods spread throughout the core. The operators of the power station will regulate the output of the reactor minute by minute by adjusting the positions of the rods, moving them in and out as the reactor is running to produce higher or lower levels of power output. The rate at which the fission process is taking place in the

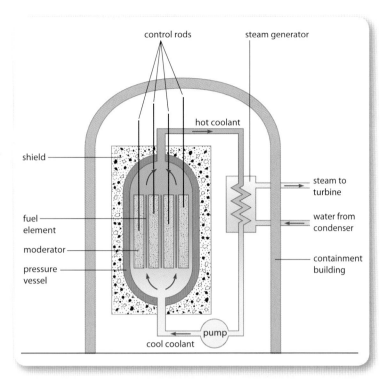

■ Cross-section of a reactor

reactor core is determined by measuring the number of neutrons present in different parts of the reactor. The temperature and pressure of the coolant are also measured.

Shutdown rods

In addition to the control rods, a reactor is also equipped with shutdown rods. These are absorbers that are either kept out of the core (when the reactor is running) or in the core (when the reactor has been shut down). The shutdown rods are controlled independently and used to stop the chain reactions rapidly in the event of an emergency.

Fission product heating

Even when the reactor has been shut down, it will still continue to produce heat. The chain reaction can be stopped by using control rods, but there is no way to stop the natural breakdown of the radioactive materials. This heat is called fission product heating. If steps are not taken to remove this heat the fuel may melt. It is essential that the reactor core is cooled at all times, even when it is not producing energy. Emergency core-cooling systems are kept ready for use in case the main cooling system fails.

REACTOR SYSTEMS

There are several different designs of nuclear power station around the world. Here, we shall look at the more common types.

■ Dismantling one of Britain's out-dated Magnox reactors is a lengthy and hazardous process.

Advanced gas-cooled reactors (AGRs)

AGRs supply over half of the electricity produced by nuclear **reactors** in Britain. The AGR is the successor to the Magnox reactor, the first type to be built in Britain, in the 1960s. Magnox reactors produced low temperature steam and were rather inefficient. In May 2000 it was confirmed that all of Britain's Magnox reactors were to be shut down.

AGRs use enriched uranium dioxide as their fuel. This can be made into a ceramic and it has a melting temperature of over 2000°C (3632°F). As the name suggests, AGRs use gas (carbon dioxide) as their coolant. The core of an AGR is made from blocks of graphite through which cylindrical cooling channels are cut. The fuel elements are placed in these channels and coolant flows through the channels. The heat output of an AGR is around 1500 megawatts and from this it produces 600 megawatts of electricity, making it about 40 per cent efficient (600 being 40 per cent of 1500). This output is similar to that of a **fossil fuel** power station.

The pressure vessel is made of special concrete around four to six metres thick, with a thin lining of stainless steel to stop the coolant gas from escaping. After heating, the coolant gas is pumped to the steam generators, which are set in the walls of the concrete pressure vessel. Once the steam has been generated, the coolant is recycled to the reactor core. The steam produced goes to a steam **turbine** for electricity production.

Pressurized water reactors (PWRs)

PWRs are the most commonly used in the world. They use normal water as both their coolant and their **moderator**. Because water absorbs **neutrons**, PWRs use enriched uranium.

The PWR uses uranium dioxide **fuel rods** clad in zirconium alloy, which resists corrosion by the water and does not absorb neutrons. The core of a PWR reactor is smaller than that of an AGR. Some of the fuel rods are left out to make room for the control and shutdown rods, which move up and down within the fuel elements. The whole core is enclosed by a 20 centimetre (8 inch) thick steel pressure vessel. PWRs have a heat output of about 3000 megawatts and an electrical output of 1000 megawatts.

The PWR has no cooling channels and the fuel elements are packed closely together. The coolant passes up through the core between the fuel rods and is then pumped to a steam generator. After transferring its heat, the coolant is pumped back to the reactor. Each reactor has three or four of these cooling cycles.

To maintain a constant coolant pressure there is a pressurizer, with a pressure release valve in case the pressure gets too high. This is an essential part of the power station – if it goes wrong it can be disastrous.

The reactor and the cooling systems are enclosed within a containment building with concrete walls about a metre thick. This is necessary because if the cooling system burst open, the high-pressure water inside would turn to steam instantly. This would cause a huge increase in pressure inside the building that could rupture the walls.

■ A PWR nuclear power station in California, USA.

FAST BREEDERS, FAST MOVERS

Fast breeder **reactors** are used to produce new fissile material in the form of plutonium. A fast breeder reactor can produce as much fuel as it consumes. This is possible because when uranium 238 absorbs a **neutron** during the operation of a reactor, it is converted into plutonium 239, which is a fissionable **isotope** and can itself be used to fuel reactors.

A typical breeder reactor has an inner core, consisting of a large number of stainless-steel tubes filled with a mixture of uranium **oxide** and plutonium oxide. This is surrounded by an outer blanket of tubes of natural uranium oxide. This breeding blanket, as it is called, captures neutrons that escape from the core and the uranium is converted into plutonium. As in other reactors, heat is removed from the core by a liquid coolant and used to produce steam, which powers a **turbine** that drives an electrical generator.

The core of a fast breeder reactor is very small as it has no **moderator**. A core 2.5 metres (8 feet) in diameter and 1.5 metres (5 feet) high will produce 1000 megawatts of electricity. It also produces a great deal of heat – around three and a half times the output of a PWR. Liquid sodium is commonly used as a coolant. It transfers heat efficiently and, unlike water, does not readily absorb neutrons. The **heat energy** produced by the reactor core is so high that the fuel would melt in seconds if the coolant stopped flowing for any reason. As extra protection the whole core is placed in a pool of liquid sodium into which heat can pass if the coolant system fails.

■ The reactor room at Beloyarskaya fast breeder in Russia

■ An experimental fast breeder reactor site in the United States

Shutdowns

The world's first commercial fast breeder was the Superphénix, built in France. It began to produce electricity in 1986, but it has been plagued by shutdowns since. The technology is controversial.

In the United States environmental concerns and the fear of plutonium falling into the hands of terrorists, who might use it to produce nuclear weapons, have halted the development of breeder reactors. Congress cut off its funding of breeder technology development in 1983. Britain shut down its prototype breeder reactor in 1994. Japan has continued its breeder development programme. In December 1995 its prototype breeder, Monju, suffered a ruptured pipe in a secondary cooling system that spilled an estimated two to five tonnes of liquid sodium which then caught fire. The reactor is located 700 metres (2,300 feet) from an active earthquake fault.

NUCLEAR ENERGY ON THE MOVE

The United States Navy recognized the potential nuclear power offered as an energy source. Under the direction of Hyman Rickover, a programme to develop a naval reactor was launched in the late 1940s. In 1954 the first nuclear submarine, the *Nautilus*, was launched. It was a complete success. Today, many of the world's navies use nuclear-powered submarines. The *Nautilus* reactor was the prototype for the first American commercial nuclear power plant, built in Shippingport, Pennsylvania, in 1957.

The *USS Triton*, launched in 1959, is propelled by two nuclear reactors. In 1960 it travelled right round the world underwater, covering 78,858 kilometres (49000 miles) in 84 days.

SPENT FUEL AND REPROCESSING

Nuclear fuel lasts for about six years in a **reactor**. After it is removed, it is called spent fuel. This spent fuel consists of uranium, various **isotopes** of plutonium and a variety of **fission** products. It is extremely hazardous, being about 100 million times more **radioactive** than fresh fuel. Most of this **radioactivity** is due to the fission products which are themselves **decaying** and emitting **radiation** as they do so. There are two ways to deal with the spent fuel. It can either be stored or it can be reprocessed.

Reprocessing

After its removal from the reactor, spent fuel is stored in water ponds 10 metres (33 feet) deep on the reactor site. It is kept here for a year or so to allow some of the shorter-lived fission products to decay. This makes it slightly less hazardous for the workers who will handle it later. The water also cools the fuel. Some fission products leak through holes in the **cladding** and **contaminate** the surrounding water, so that the water becomes low-level radioactive waste itself and needs to be disposed of.

The spent fuel has to be transported to a reprocessing plant. The safety of the flasks used to transport the fuel is a cause for concern to many. In one rather spectacular test a transport flask was placed in front of a 140 tonne locomotive travelling at 160 kilometres (99 miles) per hour. The flask remained intact. The first stage in reprocessing is to chop up the **fuel rods** and dissolve them

■ A flask for transporting spent nuclear fuel sits on a railway carriage.

in nitric acid. This releases gaseous fission products, some of which have to be collected and disposed of. These, plus the fuel cladding, become an intermediate waste disposal problem.

The next stage is the separation of the uranium and plutonium from the fission products. A solution of the fission products then has to be stored as high-level waste. The uranium and plutonium are separated from each other. Nearly all of this material is stored. They could be used for reactor fuel at some point in the future if uranium became scarce.

Reprocessing and nuclear weapons

As we shall see later, reprocessing is the link between nuclear reactors and nuclear weapons because it provides the plutonium for weapons manufacture. The United States banned commercial fuel reprocessing in the 1970s.

■ Storage cylinders containing uranium 238 removed during the process of enriching unranium for nuclear fuel.

DEALING WITH NUCLEAR WASTE

The problem of what to do with **radioactive** waste is one of the biggest difficulties for the nuclear industry. Low-level nuclear waste consists of materials such as **contaminated** clothing, packing material, and fittings from nuclear **reactors**. Intermediate-level wastes include fuel **cladding** and wastes from fuel reprocessing and require more careful storage than low-level wastes.

Low-level nuclear wastes have been placed in concrete-lined trenches and covered with soil at waste sites. Controversially, liquid low-level wastes have simply been pumped into the sea. This caused particular outrage when wastes from the Sellafield reprocessing plant in Cumbria were pumped into the Irish Sea.

High-level waste disposal

High-level waste includes spent **fuel rods** and **fission** products, such as plutonium. Spent fuel produces so much heat that it has to be cooled for decades and requires elaborate storage.

Disposal of wastes should be distinguished from storage. Stored wastes are kept safe and accessible for up to a hundred years, for possible future treatment or use. Disposal means that the wastes are put safely out of reach, with no plans for their recovery. The current preference is to dispose of high-level waste by burying it in deep underground tunnels. The waste may or may not have been reprocessed.

■ Spent nuclear fuel is encased in glass in the vitrification cell of a reprocessing plant.

■ Yucca Mountain, Nevada, where the US government plans to build a nuclear waste depository

First the waste is vitrified (encased in a special highly resistant glass). Next, cylinders of the vitrified waste are encased in 25-centimetre (10-inch) thick stainless steel containers. These containers can then be placed in underground shafts and tunnels between 300 to 1000 metres deep. The tunnels are then backfilled with clay and other materials that prevent water from getting at the containers. The tunnel walls may also be lined with concrete as a further barrier. The final barrier is the hundreds of metres of rock between the depository and the surface.

Until such sites become a reality, nuclear power stations could become simply waste-holding facilities storing the contaminated remnants of their reactor plants, as well as the spent fuel. The US Department of Energy was required to begin accepting spent nuclear fuel for disposal in January 1998, but it will be at least 2010 before its fuel burial site in Yucca Mountain, Nevada, is ready.

HOW LONG TO STORE?

It is very difficult to say how quickly radioactive wastes **decay**. There will be a range of different radioactive **isotopes** present, each with a different **half-life**, and each decaying into new radioactive isotopes which themselves will have different half-lives. Storing the wastes for 10 years will reduce **radioactivity** significantly and there is a rapid fall between 100 and 1000 years after which the isotopes decay slowly. Spent fuel has to be kept cooled for decades until the shorter half-life isotopes have decayed. It must be kept out of contact with the rest of the environment for hundreds of years at the very least.

DISPOSAL DILEMMA

A major problem in disposing of nuclear waste lies in finding a suitable site. Most people do not want to live near a waste dump, especially a waste dump containing materials they believe to be harmful. No matter how much the industry or government might protest that the waste is safely locked away, there would still be opposition.

■ A train-load of nuclear waste on its way to a disposal site passes the village of Seascale in Cumbria.

Can we be certain?

Can scientists ever say with absolute certainty that a waste disposal site will remain secure over thousands of years? The answer would have to be, 'No'. Nuclear waste has to be kept isolated for a thousand years at the very least and it is very difficult to predict how conditions will change over such a long period. This makes assessing potential waste sites a particularly difficult task. For a small country, such as Britain with its high population density, there may be no acceptable sites for high-level waste disposal. Many people believe that, at present, we have no real solution to the problem of nuclear waste and it seems that, for the foreseeable future, vitrified high-level waste will be disposed of near the surface.

A wider problem

Of course, nuclear waste disposal is by no means the only disposal problem we have to face. We are rapidly running out of places to put new landfill sites for the millions of tonnes of household and industrial waste we generate. Many people believe that the haphazard "disposal" of carbon dioxide waste from **fossil fuel** power stations and other sources into the atmosphere is leading to global climate changes. Better management of hazardous wastes of all kinds is an issue that has to be faced.

To reprocess or not to reprocess?

Reprocessing nuclear waste actually creates an even larger volume of waste that has to be disposed of. An advantage of reprocessing is that it concentrates the dangerous high-level waste into a small volume, but a major disadvantage is the large stockpiles of separated plutonium produced. There was some justification for reprocessing when the plutonium was going to be used to start fast breeder reactors, but this is no longer the case as most fast-breeder programmes have been cut back, postponed, or cancelled. For many, the hazards involved are a strong argument against reprocessing and for the long-term storage of spent fuel.

WASTE PRODUCTION

At each stage of reprocessing, wastes are produced. From the reprocessing of 4 cubic metres (5.2 cubic yards) of spent fuel from a typical PWR **reactor** 2.5 cubic metres (3.3 cubic yards) of high-level waste, 40 cubic metres (52 cubic yards) of intermediate-level waste and 600 cubic metres of low-level waste are produced. By contrast, a coal-fired power station with a similar power output leaves about 300,000 cubic metres (359,000 cubic feet) of ash that has to be disposed of.

■ Spent nuclear fuel from Japan arrives in Britain for reprocessing.

RADIATION AND LIFE

Radiation – silent, invisible, odourless, and potentially deadly – is something that we fear. Our senses give us no warning of the presence of radiation and this, perhaps, gives it a somewhat threatening and sinister aspect. So what does radiation actually do to living things?

Ionizing radiation

Broadly speaking, radiation can be divided into two groups: electromagnetic radiation, which includes radio waves, visible light, X-rays, and gamma rays, and particle radiation, such as the **neutrons**, **alpha particles** and **beta particles** given off by radioactive decay.

■ A Geiger counter is used to detect radioactivity.

Alpha and beta particles carry an electric charge. When alpha or beta particles pass through matter, the electrical forces between the particles and the **electrons** surrounding the **atoms** of the matter can be enough to push electrons from their orbits. This leaves the atom with a positive charge. This process is called ionization, and radiation that does this is called **ionizing radiation**.

Atoms are held together by bonds formed through sharing or transferring electrons. If electrons are removed by ionizing radiation then these bonds are broken and new ones may be formed. If these chemical changes take place in a living organism they can bring about biological changes that could be harmful. The amount of energy needed to cause damage to a living system is tiny. (For example, the amount of ionizing radiation needed to kill an adult human is equivalent to the energy needed to raise the body temperature by only 0.0025°C.) It is the ionization and the disruption it causes to chemical processes that does the damage.

The effect on cells

Ionizing radiation can cause damage to any part of a living **cell** but damage to the cell **nucleus** tends to be more serious, because this is where the cell's DNA is found. DNA is rather like a chemical codebook carrying the instructions the cell needs to operate efficiently. If the cell's DNA is damaged its activities will be disrupted and it may no longer be able to divide. This can have terrible effects, for example, on the cells that line the intestines. Here, cell division takes place continually as surface cells are generated to protect cells underneath. This protection will be lost if cell division ceases.

Another possibility is that the damaged cell divides uncontrollably. This can result in a cancer. Sometimes the damage done to the DNA may only become apparent if that person has children. All of the offspring's cells will carry the mutation that has been passed on by the parent. The vast majority of mutations are harmful and could result in miscarriage, stillbirth, or in the offspring being born with major life-threatening defects.

Cells do have repair mechanisms to cope with damage caused by ionizing radiation. For example, new DNA may be made to replace damaged strands. However, the repair mechanisms can fail if there is a sudden, very large dose of radiation, or if there are several doses separated by short intervals of time.

■ Workers have to wear special protective radiation suits to carry out hazardous decontamination duties.

DOSAGE AND DAMAGE

- Workers in the potentially hazardous environment of a nuclear power plant will wear "dosimeters" like this to monitor exposure to any radiation.

The type of **radiation** involved influences the damage done to living organisms. **Alpha particles** are emitted by **elements** such as uranium and plutonium. The range of an alpha particle is very short – it will not penetrate the outer skin layers – and it gives up its energy rapidly. Because they cause **ionizing** over a short distance, alpha particles are said to be densely ionizing. Damage is concentrated in a few **cells** and the damage is difficult to repair. Alpha radiation emitters are a serious hazard if they get inside the body, for example if uranium mineworkers breathe in **radioactive** dust particles.

Beta particles are high energy **electrons** and more penetrating than alpha particles. The ionizing they produce is spread over a greater distance and they are said to be lightly ionizing. The damage they cause can be more readily repaired.

Gamma radiation is highly penetrating, but only lightly ionizing. The ionization effect only occurs if the gamma rays strike **atoms**, causing them to eject electrons. Gamma rays are hazardous because they can penetrate deep into the body tissues, such as the bone marrow.

Safe levels?

Defining a safe level of exposure to any potentially damaging substance, not just radioactive ones, is very difficult. By "safe" do we mean no risk at all? This is just not practicable so we have to determine instead what level of risk is acceptable. Having done that (no easy task!), the next stage is to determine what level of radiation exposure matches the risk we are prepared to take. Again, this is not easy. At lower levels of exposure the best we can do is to say that there is some chance of a fatal cancer resulting and that risk increases with increasing exposure. What we cannot do is to state categorically that there will be this effect. The risk tables are by no means agreed upon by everyone.

Working with radioactivity

Several large-scale studies of workers in the nuclear industry have been designed to show the effects of low-level radiation exposure. However, no clear link between the incidence of cancer in radiation workers and their exposure to low-level radiation has yet been established.

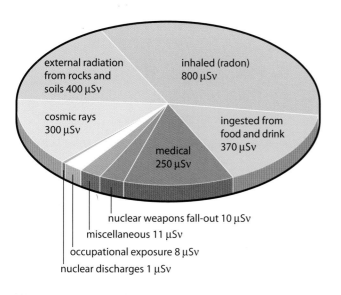

external radiation from rocks and soils 400 µSv

cosmic rays 300 µSv

inhaled (radon) 800 µSv

ingested from food and drink 370 µSv

medical 250 µSv

nuclear weapons fall-out 10 µSv
miscellaneous 11 µSv
occupational exposure 8 µSv
nuclear discharges 1 µSv

Radiation exposure is measured in sieverts (Sv). Humans can absorb 0.25 Sv without ill effects, 1.5 Sv can produce radiation sickness; 8 Sv is fatal. This chart shows exposure for the average person from various sources in millionths (µ) of Sv.

REACTOR ACCIDENTS

The biggest danger from nuclear power comes from the damaging effects of exposure to **radioactive** materials. So far, the release of **radioactivity** into the environment as a result of a major accident at a **reactor** has been a rare occurrence. But it has happened and it could happen again.

Windscale

In 1957 a fire broke out in the reactor at Windscale, Cumbria. So far, it is the most serious accident to have occurred at a reactor in Britain.

On 1 October 1957, what had been a standard operating procedure went wrong. The temperature rose in the reactor and both the graphite **moderator** and the uranium fuel caught fire. Radioactive **fission** products were released into the atmosphere and as a result milk from an area 500 square kilometres (190 square miles) around the site had to be destroyed to prevent radioactive iodine entering the human **food chain**. None of the workers were exposed to levels high enough to cause **radiation** sickness, but they, and many people living nearby, received doses far in excess of permitted levels. A full report of the accident was not made public until 1982 when a report issued by the National Radiological Protection Board suggested that an estimated 32 additional cancer deaths happened as a result of the contamination.

■ The nuclear power station at Three Mile Island, Pennsylvania

Three Mile Island

On 28 March 1979, a pump circulating cooling water in one of two PWRs at Three Mile Island, Harrisburg, Pennsylvania in the United States, stopped operating. The coolant immediately began to heat up and a few seconds later a pressure release valve in the pressurizer opened. Seconds after this, the reactor shutdown rods were deployed automatically and the **chain reaction** was stopped. Soon the coolant temperature and pressure dropped, but the pressure relief valve stayed open.

The open valve allowed water to escape from the cooling circuit. It was eventually pumped into a storage tank from which **fission** products escaped into the environment. After two minutes the falling coolant pressure triggered the emergency core cooling system. The operators, mistakenly thinking there was too much water in the core, turned the emergency cooling system off. Eventually the water in the primary cooling circuit started to boil and the **cladding** on the **fuel rods** began to melt. Adequate cooling was not re-established for 16 hours, by which time a third of the fuel had melted and the containment building was **contaminated**. The reactor was never operated again.

■ Workers at Three Mile Island practise retrieving items from a model of the damaged reactor.

EXPECTING THE UNEXPECTED

One problem that the mistakes at Three Mile Island made clear was that when accidents happen, workers may have no experience in dealing with them. Yet accidents in nuclear power stations can have such catastrophic consequences it is essential that they are dealt with efficiently. One answer is to use reactor simulators in training. A computer connected to a control console simulates the behaviour of the reactor under different circumstances, giving the operator the chance to learn how to deal with a variety of events.

CHERNOBYL AND BEYOND

The worst nuclear accident to date happened to one of the **reactors** at Chernobyl, near the Ukranian town of Pripyat in the former Soviet Union, on 26 April 1986. The Chernobyl reactor had been in operation since 1984 and was one of the Soviet Union's most successful nuclear power stations.

As part of a safety study, a test was run to determine how long the electricity generators would run if the steam supply to the **turbine** was cut off. During the test the power level fell uncontrollably to a point where the reactor was becoming unstable. The reactor should have shut down automatically, but the operators prevented this. Despite the problems, they decided to go ahead with the test and shut off the steam supply to the turbines.

Out of control

At this point only seven control rods were in the core, even though the operating instructions required a minimum of thirty. The reactor became supercritical and the control rods could not be inserted quickly enough to bring it under control. Within three to four seconds the power rose to a hundred times its maximum design level. Most of the core melted. A chemical explosion followed, as the molten fuel reacted with the cooling water and lifted the 2000-tonne reactor cap off. The building containing the reactor was blown apart. **Fission** products from the core were lifted high into the atmosphere by the hot gas and continued to stream out for 10 days before the fire was brought under control and **radioactive** material had dispersed across Europe.

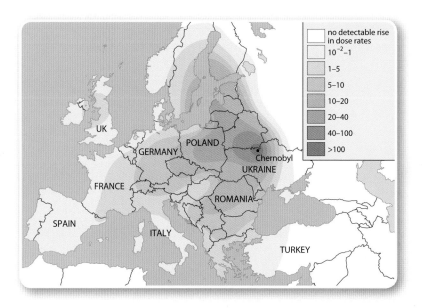

no detectable rise in dose rates	
10^{-2}–1	
1–5	
5–10	
10–20	
20–40	
40–100	
>100	

- How radiation levels rose across Europe after the Chernobyl disaster

Russia today

Sosnovy-Bor, a suburb of St Petersburg, has a digital Geiger counter on the town hall displaying local **radiation** levels in large red letters. The town's only industry is the Leningrad Nuclear Power Plant, a Chernobyl-type power station. Although the plant suffered a leak of radioactive material in 1992, it is currently being overhauled in order to extend its life for another 15 years. Many organizations have expressed doubts about the safety of the plant. If Chernobyl had happened here, many of the four million people of St Petersburg would have received a massive dose of radiation. The situation among the workers gives cause for concern too.

■ The massive damage caused by the explosion at Chernobyl is clearly shown.

Many employees don't wear any protective gear at all and workers routinely get their government salaries as much as six months late.

Most experts agree that the only way to make the reactors safe is to shut them down. The US Department of Energy has a list of the world's seven most dangerous reactors: all are in the former Soviet Union. "Many Soviet-designed reactors ... pose significant safety risks", the agency said in a 1995 report, and "these reactors continue to experience serious incidents, raising the spectre of another accident akin to Chernobyl."

COULD IT HAPPEN AGAIN?

Asked if he thought another Chernobyl could happen, a spokesman for the International Atomic Energy Agency said, "I don't think so. Safety has improved throughout the world. But there are no guarantees. And there's absolutely no reason for complacency. We have to do our best and cross our fingers." Does that sound reassuring?

NUCLEAR FUTURE

In the 1980s orders for new nuclear **reactor** constructions and for stations to start up ranged from 20 to 40 per year. In 2004 there were just two new orders, in Japan and India, and five start-ups, in China, Japan, Ukraine and Russia. It is economics, not **radiation** hazards, bringing about the end of the nuclear power industry. Nuclear power plants need increasingly expensive maintenance as they get older and it won't be easy to shut the reactors down. Around 16 per cent of the world's power now comes from nuclear plants, so alternatives will have to be found.

In a report aimed at examining the future of nuclear power in Europe, the French Senate's Delegation to the European Union warned that the EU should not risk losing its know-how in nuclear power. They pointed out how important it is for Europe. One third of Europe's electricity is generated by nuclear power; France gets about three quarters of its power from nuclear reactors. However, European countries that favour nuclear power are in the minority.

The end of the nuclear dream?

Britain became the first European country to decommission a reactor, when it decided in 1999 to shut Dounreay power station near Thurso in Scotland. The cleanup and shutdown process will take up to a hundred years and cost £500 million. The decision was made after **radioactive** particles were found on local beaches. The sand-like particles are radioactive enough to blister someone who sits on them. Officials say they don't know how they escaped.

Nuclear fusion

Nuclear **fusion** is the opposite of nuclear **fission**. Nuclear fusion occurs when the **nuclei** of two lighter **atoms** combine to form a heavier one, rather than a heavy **nucleus** splitting apart. The resulting atom has a smaller **mass** than the original ones, because some of the mass is transformed into energy.

This is the process that powers hydrogen bombs and stars. Gram for gram, fusion produces eight times more energy than the fission of uranium, and over a million times more than could be obtained by burning the same weight of **fossil fuels**. Fusion is not only desirable because it is such a wonderful energy source, but also because the fuels used (**isotopes** of hydrogen) are relatively abundant. Also, the product of the reaction is inert helium, rather than polluting gases or radioactive waste.

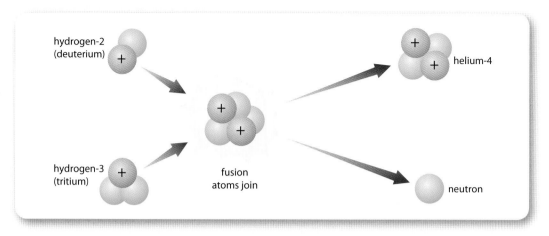

■ Two isotopes of hydrogen undergo fusion to become helium plus a neutron.

Research is being conducted on controlled fusion energy in many countries, particularly the United States, Japan, and the European Union. However, in experiments so far, the energy obtained in the laboratory has scarcely exceeded the energy put in to run the tests. Fusion reactions are difficult to achieve because the nuclei have to be made to collide at very high speeds and this requires temperatures of 100 million°C (212 million°F) or more.

Few people believe that fusion power will be available commercially at any time in the foreseeable future. The extremely high cost of fusion research, and the uncertainty of a return on the investment makes most businesses and governments very reluctant to finance its development. Co-operation among countries to share the costs may be the only way forward.

■ A nuclear fusion test reactor at Princeton University in the United States.

NUCLEAR WEAPONS

There is no better illustration of the way in which human inventiveness can be turned to a terrible purpose than nuclear weapons. The discovery that vast amounts of energy could be released by splitting the **atom** was an exciting one, opening up the possibility of a new source of power for society. However, what spurred the effort to harness atomic power was not the desire to benefit society, but to produce a bomb. The successful detonation of the first atomic bomb at Los Alamos, New Mexico, in the United States on 16 July 1945, heralded a new era in which, for decades to come, the threat of nuclear destruction would hang over the Earth.

A bigger bang

In conventional explosives a chemical reaction releases energy very rapidly. The amount of energy released depends on the **mass** of the explosive chemicals. Nuclear weapons are different, but the energy they release is often given in terms of the equivalent amount of TNT, a common explosive, needed to produce the same results.

A **fission** weapon contains pure, or nearly pure plutonium 239 or uranium enriched to over 90 per cent U235. Around the outside of the bomb is a layer of conventional explosives. When the explosives are triggered the fissile material is compressed, making it supercritical and bringing about a runaway **chain reaction** within millionths of a second.

■ An American airman surveys the devastation caused by the atomic bomb at Hiroshima.

A **fusion** weapon uses the power of a fission bomb to provide the energy needed to heat up and compress **isotopes** of hydrogen so that they fuse together, releasing devastating amounts of energy. Because fusion weapons use hydrogen, they are often referred to as hydrogen bombs or H bombs.

Weapons production

If a country wants to build nuclear weapons it needs a supply of fissile material. This means having either a uranium enrichment facility or a nuclear **reactor** to produce plutonium and a reprocessing plant to extract it. The amount of plutonium needed to make a weapon varies, but 10 kilograms (22 pounds) is average. Quite small reactors, not designed to produce electricity, can be used for weapons production.

The International Atomic Energy Agency monitors the use of nuclear technology to make sure that it is only used for peaceful purposes. It sometimes sends inspectors to countries to make sure that they are not building nuclear weapons. Currently many countries are concerned that Iran and North Korea may be using their nuclear technology to develop weapons.

NUCLEAR COUNTRIES

There are a number of countries that have nuclear power, but do not (so far as we know) have nuclear weapons. These include Canada, Japan, Sweden, and the Netherlands. Israel, however, has nuclear weapons but no nuclear power.

■ Tension between India and Pakistan grew in 1998 when India conducted five underground nuclear weapons tests near the Pakistan border.

43

TIMELINE

1896 French physicist Antoine Henri Becquerel discovers radioactivity

1905 Albert Einstein shows that **mass** and energy can be converted from one to the other

1919 New Zealand physicist Ernest Rutherford splits the **atom**, by bombarding a nitrogen **nucleus** with **alpha particles**

1939 Otto Hahn, Fritz Strassmann and Lise Meitner announce the discovery of nuclear **fission**

1942 Enrico Fermi builds the first nuclear reactor, in a squash court at the University of Chicago, USA

1945 The first atom bomb is detonated at Los Alamos, New Mexico

1951 The Experimental Breeder Reactor, Idaho, USA, produces the first electricity to be generated by **nuclear energy**

1956 The world's first commercial nuclear power station, Calder Hall, comes into operation in the UK

1957 Release of radiation from Windscale (now Sellafield) nuclear power station, Cumbria, England. In Kyshtym, USSR, escape of plutonium waste caused an unknown number of casualties. On maps produced the following year 30 small communities had been deleted.

1979 Nuclear-reactor accident at Three Mile Island, Pennsylvania, USA

1986 Explosion in a reactor at Chernobyl results in clouds of radioactive material spreading as far as Sweden

1991 The first controlled production of nuclear-fusion energy is achieved at the Joint European Torus (JET), Culham, Oxfordshire, England

1995 Sizewell B, the UK's first pressurized-water nuclear reactor and the most advanced nuclear power station in the world, begins operating in Suffolk, England

1997 English physicists at JET produce a record 12 megawatts of nuclear-**fusion** power

1999 Japan's worst-ever nuclear accident results in 49 people, mostly plant workers, being exposed to potentially harmful levels of **radiation**

2006 The first generation of nuclear reactors are coming to the end of their life and are being decommissioned. Will governments build a new generation of reactors, or will we have to find the energy from somewhere else?

INTERNATIONAL NUCLEAR EVENT SCALE

The International Nuclear Event Scale (INES) was designed to communicate to the public the safety issues of reported events at nuclear installations. There are seven levels, with level 7 the most dangerous.

7 Major accident
Example: Chernobyl, USSR (now Ukraine), 1986.

6 Serious accident
Example: Kyshtym Reprocessing Plant, USSR (now Russia), 1957.

5 Accident with off-site risk
Examples: Windscale Pile, UK, 1957; Three Mile Island, USA, 1979.

4 Accident without significant off-site risk
Windscale Reprocessing Plant, UK, 1973; Saint-Laurent NPP, France, 1980; Buenos Aires Critical Assembly, Argentina, 1983.

3 Serious incident
Example: Vandellos NPP, Spain, 1989.

2 Incident

FIND OUT MORE

There is plenty of information on the Internet and in books if you want to learn more about nuclear energy. Use a search engine such as *www.google.com* to search for information. A search for the words "nuclear energy" will bring back lots of results, but it may be difficult to find the information you want. Try refining your search to look for some of the people and things mentioned in this book, such as "Albert Einstein" or "Chernobyl".

More Books to Read

Graham, Ian. *Energy Forever: Nuclear Power*. London: Hodder Wayland, 2001

Saunders, Nigel and Steven Chapman. *Energy Essentials: Nuclear Energy*, Oxford: Raintree, 2004

Websites

www.sciencemuseum.org.uk/exhibitions/energy
Discover loads of information and activities about different sources of energy.

www.greenpeace.org
This is the website for an environmental pressure group. You will find information about the environmental impact of nuclear power. Remember that organizations in favour of nuclear power might present this information very differently.

GLOSSARY

alpha particle   positively charged, high energy particle consisting of two protons and two neutrons emitted from the nucleus of a radioactive atom. Releasing an alpha particle transforms one element into another as the atomic number is reduced by two.

atomic energy   see nuclear energy

atomic number   number of protons in the nucleus of an atom. Every element has a different atomic number.

atoms   smallest units of matter that can take part in a chemical reaction, and the smallest parts of an element that can exist

beta particle   electron ejected at high speed from the nucleus of a radioactive atom. They are created when a neutron changes into a proton, emitting an electron as it does so.

boron   chemical element used in the making of control rods for nuclear reactors because of its ability to absorb neutrons

cells   smallest units of life capable of independent existence. All living things, with the exception of viruses, consist of one or more cells.

chain reaction   fission reaction in which neutrons released by the splitting of atomic nuclei strike other nuclei causing them to split and release more neutrons, which cause still more nuclei to split, and so on

chemical energy   energy held in the bonds that hold atoms together in molecules. Chemical energy is released during a chemical reaction.

cladding   metal covering around a rod or pellet of nuclear fuel

contaminate   to make impure by adding unwanted or undesirable substances

decay   the disintegration of the nuclei of radioactive elements

diffuse   to mingle with another substance through the movement of particles

electron   one of the subatomic particles that make up an atom. Electrons have a negative electric charge and orbit around the central nucleus of the atom.

element   substance that cannot be split into a simpler substance by means of a chemical reaction

fission   splitting of a large atomic nucleus into two or more smaller nuclei

food chain   feeding pathway by which energy and mass is passed from one living organism to another

fossil fuels   fuels produced through the action of heat and pressure on the fossil remains of plants and animals that lived millions of years ago. Fossil fuels include coal, petroleum and natural gas.

fuel rod   rod or pellet of fissile material, usually uranium, together with its protective cladding, used to power a nuclear reactor

fusion   process by which two small atomic nuclei combine to produce a single larger nucleus with the release of a great deal of energy

gamma radiation   high energy, short wavelength electromagnetic radiation released from a radioactive atom

half-life   time it takes for half of a quantity of a radioactive substance to decay. Half-lives can vary from billionths of a second to billions of years.

heat energy   energy associated with the motion of atoms and molecules

ionizing radiation   radiation that knocks electrons from atoms, leaving positively charged ions in its path

isotopes atoms that have the same number of protons (and are therefore of the same chemical element) but which have different numbers of neutrons and so have different atomic masses

mass the amount of matter in an object

meltdown accident in a nuclear reactor in which the reactor core melts as a result of the fuel overheating

moderator material used in a nuclear reactor to reduce the speed of high-energy neutrons and so control the rate at which energy is produced

molecule two or more atoms joined together by chemical bonds; if the atoms are the same it is an element, if they are different it is a compound

neutron one of the subatomic particles that make up an atom. Neutrons have no electric charge and are found in the central nucleus of the atom.

nuclear energy (also called atomic energy) energy in the nucleus of an atom released when a large nucleus breaks down into two smaller nuclei (fission) or when two small nuclei combine to form a larger nucleus (fusion)

nucleus central part of an atom, made up of protons and neutrons and containing nearly all of the atom's mass

oxide compound that contains oxygen

proton one of the subatomic particles that make up an atom. Protons are in the central nucleus of the atom and have a positive electric charge.

radiation energy given off in the form of fast-moving particles or electromagnetic waves as a result of the decay of an atomic nucleus

radioactive describes a substance that gives off radiation

radioactivity the release of radiation from a substance in the forms of alpha and beta particles and gamma rays

reactor structure in which radioactive material is made to break down in a controlled way, releasing energy that can be put to use

turbine engine in which a fluid is used to spin a shaft by pushing on angled blades like those on a fan. Turbines are used to spin generators for producing electricity.

INDEX

accidents 5, 25, 36–39, 44
advanced gas-cooled reactors (AGRs) 22–23
alpha particles 9, 32, 34
Atomic Energy Commission (AEC) 13
atomic numbers 6, 7
atoms 4, 6–7, 8, 9, 10, 11, 12, 16, 32, 40, 42

beta particles 9, 32, 34
birth defects 33
boron 11, 20

cancer 33, 35, 36
cell damage 33, 34
chain reactions 10–11, 19, 20, 21, 37, 42
chemical energy 8
chemical reactions 6, 8, 42
Chernobyl 38, 39, 44
cladding 18, 20, 26, 27, 28, 37
contamination 26, 28, 29, 36, 37
control rods 11, 20, 21, 23, 38
coolants 18, 19, 20, 21, 22, 23, 24, 37
critical mass 11

DNA 33

Einstein, Albert 4, 8
electricity 4, 9, 13, 22, 40
electromagnetic radiation 9, 32
electrons 6, 9, 32, 34
elements 6, 7, 8, 12, 14, 15, 34
energy 4, 8, 9, 32, 40, 41, 42
environmental issues 25, 30, 31
ethical issues 15

fast breeder reactors 24–25, 31
fission 10, 11, 12, 13, 18, 21, 42
fission products 11, 20, 26, 27, 28, 36, 37, 38
food chain 36
fossil fuels 4, 8, 14, 18, 31, 41
fuel rods 18, 20, 23, 27, 28, 37
fusion 40–41, 43

gamma radiation 8, 9, 19, 34
gas centrifuge enrichment 17
gas diffusion 13, 16

half-life 7, 29
heat energy 9, 24
hydrogen 6, 7, 8, 19, 43

International Nuclear Event Scale (INES) 44
ionization 32, 34
ionizing radiation 32, 33
isotopes 7, 10, 13, 15, 19, 24, 26, 29, 41, 43

kinetic energy 9

Manhattan Project 12, 13
mass 4, 8, 40
meltdown 5
moderators 19
molecules 16, 17

neutrons 6, 7, 8, 9, 10, 11, 12, 19, 20, 21, 23, 24, 32
nuclear energy 4, 13, 18, 40
nuclear fuel production 16–17
nuclear power plants 10, 13, 18–25, 40
nuclear reactions 8
nuclear submarines 25
nuclear waste 4, 26–31
nuclear weapons 5, 12, 13, 27, 41, 42–43
nuclei 6, 7, 8, 9, 10, 11, 13, 19, 33, 40, 41

particle radiation 32
plutonium 13, 24, 25, 26, 27, 28, 31, 34, 42, 43
pressurized water reactors (PWRs) 23, 37
protons 6, 7, 9, 19

radiation 5, 15, 32–35
radiation exposure 5, 15, 35
radiation sickness 36
radioactivity 4, 5, 7, 8, 9, 15, 20, 21, 26, 32, 34, 36, 38, 40, 44
radon 15
reactors 4, 5, 11, 12, 13, 16, 18, 19, 20, 21, 22–25, 26, 28, 31, 36, 37, 38, 39, 40, 43
relativity theory 4, 8
reprocessing 26-7, 28, 31, 43

safety 5, 15, 16, 19, 26, 35, 39, 44
shielding 19
shutdown rods 21, 23, 37
spent fuel 26, 28, 29, 31

Three Mile Island 37, 44

uranium 6, 7, 9, 10, 11, 12, 13, 14–15, 16, 23, 24, 26, 27, 28, 34, 42
uranium dioxide 16, 17, 22, 23
uranium mines 14–15
uranium oxide 14, 24

Windscale 36, 43, 44